# CHRISTMAS CRACKER JOKES

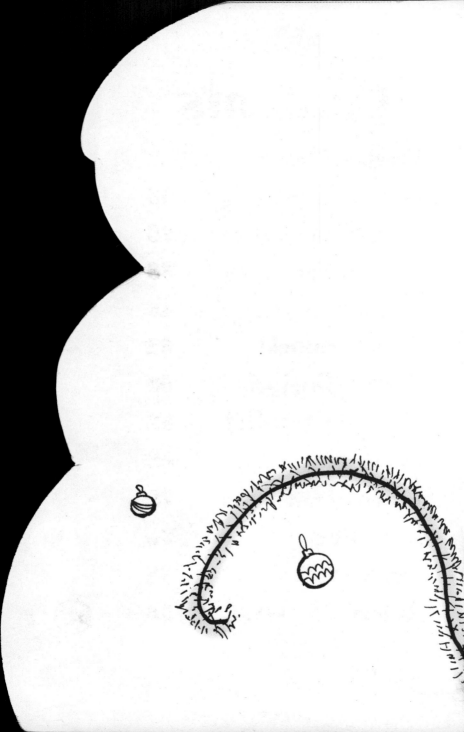

# CHRISTMAS CRACKER JOKES

What food should you never trust at Christmas?

Mince spies.

First published 2018 by Macmillan Children's Books
an imprint of Pan Macmillan
20 New Wharf Road, London N1 9RR
Associated companies throughout the world
www.panmacmillan.com

ISBN 978-1-5290-0355-0

Text copyright © Macmillan Children's Books 2018

1 3 5 7 9 8 6 4 2

A CIP catalogue record for this book is available from
the British Library.

Compiled and illustrated by Perfect Bound Ltd
Illustrated by Dan Newman and Grace Newman
Printed and bound by CPI Group (UK) Ltd, Croydon CRO 4YY

# Contents

# Cracker Classics

What do trees do
on the internet?

**They log on.**

Who built the
Round Table for
King Arthur?

**Sir Cumference.**

What did one traffic
light say to the other?

**'Don't look! I'm
changing.'**

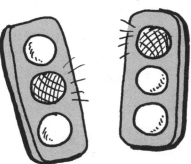

What does the sea say
to the beach?

**Nothing – it just waves.**

What did the envelope
say to the stamp?

**'Stick with me
and we'll go places.'**

Why can't bicycles stand up on their own?

**Because they're two-tyred.**

Why do bakers charge so much for bread?

**Because they knead the dough.**

Thanks for explaining the word 'many' to me . . .

**. . . it means a lot.**

I went to the zoo. They had a baguette in a cage. It was bread in captivity.

How does a gardener fix a hole in his jeans?

With a vegetable patch.

What kind of flowers grow on your face?

Two-lips.

Where should you
take a sick flower?

**Hospetal.**

Why did my dad get fired
from the banana factory?

**He kept chucking out
the bent ones.**

I got a massive lump of
plasticine for Christmas.

**I don't know what to
make of it.**

Last night I prepared
a candlelit dinner.

It was terrible – barely
cooked and all smoky.

What are invisible
and smell of
bananas?

Monkey burps.

What should you do if
you see a spaceman?

Park in it, man.

I stayed up all night,
wondering where
the sun had gone.

Eventually, it
dawned on me.

I went window-shopping
at the weekend.

I bought thirty windows.

I regret buying that
ice-cream van.

It melted.

Why did the Jelly
Baby go to school?

Because he wanted
to be a Smartie.

What's the difference
between a bus driver
and a cold?

One knows the stops,
and the other stops
the nose.

Why did the child eat
a pound coin?

Because his mum said it
was his dinner money.

My cousin is named
after his father.
He's called 'Dad'.

What's the hardest part
of making chocolate
chip cookies?

Peeling all the Smarties.

How do you make antifreeze?

Hide her woolly jumper.

Did you hear about the cowboy who wore paper boots, paper jeans, a paper shirt and a paper hat?

He was arrested for rustling.

Thieves have stolen two baths and a shower.
They made a clean getaway.

What do burglars have at bedtime?
Milk and crookies.

I slept like a baby last night.
I woke up crying every two hours.

I went to the gym to learn how to weightlift.

I'm beginning to pick it up.

For some reason, I can only remember twenty-five letters of the alphabet.

I don't know Y.

I put a whiteboard
and rows of desks
in my bedroom.
**It looks really classy.**

Yesterday I fell
down a deep
dark hole.

**I didn't see
that well.**

Whenever I ride my
bike, I ride it twice.
**I'm very keen on
recycling.**

I told my mum she'd drawn her eyebrows on too high.
**She looked pretty surprised.**

I wanted to make a ballet skirt, but I didn't know where to start.
**Then I put tu and tu together.**

What do hippies do?
**They hold your leggies on.**

What's green and
furry, has six legs
and can't swim?

**A pool table.**

My granny's
very tall and
thin, with a big
round head.

**She's a lollipop
lady.**

What's round,
bright and silly?
**A fool moon.**

What do you call
a lost meteorite?
**A meteowrong.**

Where does a general
keep his armies?
**Up his sleevies.**

# Food Funnies

What did the fast-walking tomato say to the slow-walking tomato?

**Ketchup!**

What do you give to a sick lemon?

**Lemonaid.**

What's miserable and covered in custard?

**Apple grumble.**

What is square and yellow?

**A lemon in disguise.**

What do you call fake spaghetti?

**An impasta.**

Which cheese do you use
to encourage a bear?
**Camembert.**

Which cheese is
not yours?
**Nacho cheese.**

What kind of cheese is
made backwards?
**Edam.**

What does cheese
say when it looks
in the mirror?

**Halloumi.**

Which cheese do
you use to disguise
a small horse?

**Mascarpone.**

How do you handle
dangerous cheese?

**Caerphilly.**

What colour is a burp?

**Burple.**

Why did the jelly wobble?

**It saw the milkshake.**

What's the fastest vegetable?

**A runner bean.**

What's green and goes 'boing, boing'?

**A spring onion.**

What vegetable is always wet?

**A leek.**

Why did the orange take the day off school?

**It wasn't peeling well.**

Name two things
you can't eat for
breakfast.

**Lunch and dinner.**

What's small, red
and whispers?

**A hoarse radish.**

What
happened
to the grape
when it was
stepped on?

**It let out a little
whine.**

What's a dog's favourite pizza?

**Pupperoni.**

Where do tough chickens come from?

**Hard-boiled eggs.**

# Christmas Quips

What do you
get if you eat
Christmas
decorations?

**Tinsillitis!**

Mum asked Dad for
some diamonds for
Christmas . . .

He bought her
a pack of cards.

Who delivers presents
to all the pets?

Santa Paws.

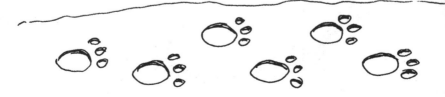

Who do Father Christmas's helpers work for?

No one. They're elf-employed.

What kind of photos do Father Christmas's helpers take?

Elfies.

Why does Father Christmas only go down chimneys and not through front doors?

**Because of elf and safety regulations.**

What is an elf's favourite vehicle?

**A mini.**

What do you call Father Christmas on holiday?

**Sandy Claus.**

What's red and white and smells?

**Farter Christmas.**

What is a mummy's
favourite part of
Christmas?

**Wrapping presents.**

What did one snowman
say to the other?

**Ice to meet you.**

What do you call
a snow house
with no loo?

**An ig.**

Who brings presents to
the seacreatures?

**Santa Jaws.**

Snowmen keep
ignoring me . . .
**I wish they'd stop
giving me the cold
shoulder!**

What's the coldest
time of year?
**Decembrrrrrr.**

What food should you never trust at Christmas?

**Mince spies.**

Why was the snowman looking at carrots in the supermarket?

**He was picking his nose.**

Why are Christmas trees so bad at knitting?

Because they keep dropping their needles.

Father Christmas has a reindeer with three humps on his back.

He's called Humphrey.

35

# Frightful Funnies

Why do all witches look the same?

**Because you can't tell which witch is which.**

What do witches use to wrap presents?

**Spellotape.**

How do you make a witch itch?

Take away the 'w'.

What do witches use to stay pale in the summer?

Suntan potion.

Why are ghosts so
bad at lying?

You can see right
through them.

How do ghosts
like their eggs?

Terrorfried.

What do ghosts
eat for dinner?

**Spookhetti.**

And what do ghosts
eat for pudding?

**I scream.**

Where do phantoms
buy stamps?

**At the ghost office.**

39

Why didn't the skeleton
go to the party?
He had no body
to go with.

How do
skeletons
catch up with
friends?
By mobile
bone.

How can you tell there's a
baby skeleton nearby?
You can hear its rattle.

Do all zombies
have girlfriends?
Only the good-
lurking ones.

On what day do
monsters eat people?
Chewsday.

What do you say
to a monster with
three heads?

**'Hello, hello, hello!'**

What do you do if a
monster knocks
on your door?

**Don't answer it.**

Where does a monster
sit on the train?

**Anywhere she likes!**

What's a sea monster's
favourite meal?

**Fish and ships.**

What's hairy, scary and goes up and down?

**A monster on a trampoline.**

What do you give a seasick monster?

**Plenty of room.**

Which monster
loves dancing?
**The boogieman.**

Who is the
cleverest monster?
**Frank Einstein.**

How do ghosts go
on holiday?
**By scaroplane.**

# Dippy Dinosaurs

What do you call a sleeping dinosaur?

**A stegosnorus.**

What do you call a wet dinosaur?

**A driplodocus.**

What do you call a
destructive dinosaur?
**Tyrannosaurus
wrecks.**

What makes more noise
than a hungry dinosaur?
**Two hungry dinosaurs.**

What do triceratops sit on?
**Tricerabottoms.**

Which dinosaurs
could jump higher
than a house?

All of them –
houses can't jump.

What do you call a
T-rex with a banana
in each ear?

Anything you like –
it can't hear you.

Which was the scariest dinosaur?
The terrordactyl.

What did dinosaurs have that no other creature has?

Baby dinosaurs.

Do you know how long dinosaurs roamed the earth?

Exactly the same way as short dinosaurs.

What dinosaur
never gives up?

**The try-try-tryceratops.**

What do you call a
one-eyed dinosaur?

**Doyouthinkhesaurus.**

What do you call a one-
eyed dinosaur's dog?

**Doyouthinkhesaurus rex.**

Why do they have
old dinosaur bones
in the museum?

**They can't afford
new ones.**

What do you get when
a T-rex sneezes?

**Out of the way.**

# Knock, Knock!

Knock, knock!
Who's there?
Interrupting cow.
Interrup—

MOOOO!

Knock, knock!
Who's there?
Europe.
Europe who?
No I'm not!

Knock, knock!
Who's there?
Hatch.
Hatch who?
Bless you!

Knock, knock!
Who's there?
Lettuce.
Lettuce who?
Lettuce in please!

Knock, knock!
Who's there?
Cows go.
Cows go who?
No, they go 'moo', silly!

Knock, knock!
Who's there?
Boo.
Boo who?
Don't cry,
it's only a joke!

Knock, knock!
Who's there?
Eye nose.
Eye nose
who?
Eye nose
loads of
jokes like
this!

Knock, knock!
Who's there?
Ivor Dunnup.
Ivor Dunnup who?
I wondered what the
smell was!

Knock, knock!
Who's there?
Wooden shoe.
Wooden shoe who?
Wooden shoe like to hear
another joke?

Knock, knock!
Who's there?
Tank.
Tank who?
You're welcome.

Knock, knock!
Who's there?
Avenue.
Avenue who?
Avenue realized it's
me yet?

Knock, knock!
Who's there?
Eva.
Eva who?
Eva you let me in
or I call the police.

Knock, knock!
Who's there?
Police.
Police who?
Police will you let me in!

# Doctor, Doctor!

Doctor, doctor,
I'm frightened of
two-letter words!

Really?

Yes, I can't even
think about it.

Doctor, doctor, I've
been stung by a bee!

Do you want me to put
some cream on it?

Don't be silly. It'll be
miles away by now.

Doctor, doctor,
I think I'm a dustbin!
Oh, you're full
of rubbish.

Doctor, doctor,
everyone ignores me.
Next patient, please!

Doctor, doctor, I'm losing
my memory.
I see. When did this start?
When did what start?

Doctor, doctor, I think I'm a pair of curtains!

You need to pull yourself together.

Doctor, doctor, I've just been beaten up by an enormous insect!

I think there's a nasty bug going round.

Doctor, doctor, I've got a sausage up my nose and mash in my ears!

I don't think you've been eating properly.

Doctor, doctor, I've hurt my arm in two places!

Well don't go back to those places again.

# What Do You Get . . .

What do you get if you cross a sheep with a kangaroo?

**A woolly jumper.**

What do you get if you cross a parrot with a centipede?

**A walkie-talkie.**

What do you get if
you cross a kangaroo
with an elephant?

**Massive holes all
over Australia.**

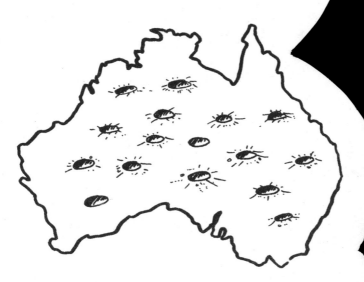

What do you get if you
cross a blue cat with
a red parrot?

**A purple carrot.**

What do you get if
you cross a snake with
a hedgehog?

**Barbed wire.**

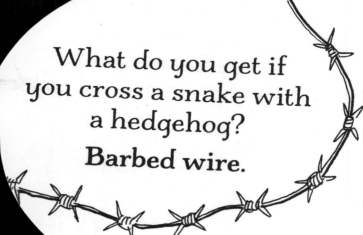

What do you get if you
cross a turkey with
an octopus?

**Enough drumsticks for
everyone at Christmas.**

What do you
get if you cross
a chicken with a
cement mixer?

**A brick layer.**

What do you get
if you cross ten
cars with some
strawberries?

**A traffic jam.**

What do you get if you
cross a cheetah with
a hamburger?

**Really fast food.**

What do you get
if you cross an
elephant with a fish?

**Swimming trunks.**

What do you get if
you cross a pudding
with a cowpat?

**A smelly jelly.**

What do you get if
you cross a cuddly
toy with a fridge?

A teddy brrrrr.

What do you get if
you cross a cocker
spaniel, a poodle
and a rooster?

A cockerpoodledoo.

# Fairy Tales

Who shouted
'Bum!' at the Big
Bad Wolf?
Little Rude Riding
Hood.

IIRFPHT

What pet did
Aladdin have?
A flying carpet.

Who flies through the
air in his underwear?

Peter Pants.

Why do dragons
sleep all day?

So they can fight
knights.

How does Captain Hook
wake up in the morning?

He has an alarm croc.

Why is Cinderella so
bad at football?

She keeps running
away from the ball.

Why would Snow
White make a
good judge?

Because she is the
fairest of them all.

Who is the funniest
princess?

**RaPUNzel.**

Which fairy is
the smelliest?

**Stinkerbell.**

Who is beautiful,
grey and wears
glass slippers?

**Cinderelephant.**

# Creepy-crawlies

What do you call
an evil insect?
**A baddy-long-legs.**

MWAH HAH HAAH

What did the
grumpy bee say?
**'Buzz off!'**

What's black and
yellow and goes
'zzub, zzub'?

A bee flying backwards.

What is the largest
kind of ant?

A giant.

Where do you take
a sick insect?

**To the waspital.**

Why couldn't the
centipede be in the
football team?

**Because she took too
long to put her boots on.**

Why did the
fly fly?
Because the
spider spied 'er.

What's the
difference between
a fly and a bird?
A bird can fly, but a
fly can't bird.

What do bees like to chew?
Bumblegum.

Why do bees hum?

Because they've forgotten the words.

What do you call an ant with ten eyes?

Ant-ten-eye.

What do you call a fly with no wings?

A walk.

What's worse that
finding a slug in
your sandwich?

**Finding half a slug.**

How can you tell which
end of a worm is which?

**Tickle the middle and see
which end laughs.**

Where can you
find giant snails?

At the end of
giants' fingers.

What do you call two
spiders that have just
got married?

Newly-webs.

What are caterpillars
afraid of?

Dogerpillars.

How do fleas get
from dog to dog?

They itch-hike.

# Sea Sillies

Which fish goes well
with ice cream?

**A jellyfish.**

Which fish is the
most valuable?

**A goldfish.**

What is a knight's
favourite fish?

**A swordfish.**

What's the best
way to get in
touch with
a fish?

**Drop it a line.**

HELLO

Why do lobsters
not like sharing?

**Because they're
shellfish.**

How do little squids
go to school?

**By octobus.**

What do you
call a fish with
three eyes?

**Fiiish.**

How do you cut an ocean?
**With a sea-saw.**

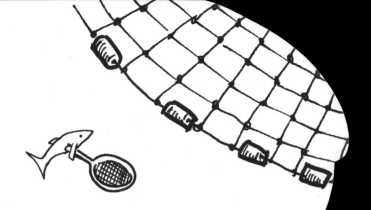

Why are fish no
good at tennis?

They don't like to get
too close to the net.

Why did the
lobster blush?

Because the seaweed!

What's the strongest creature in the sea?
**The mussel.**

What do sea creatures watch in the evening?
**Telefishion.**

What happened to the cold jellyfish?
**It set.**

What do baby sharks get before they go to sleep?

**A bite-time story.**

How do sea creatures carry big things?

**In a whalebarrow.**

What does an oyster
do on her birthday?

She shellebrates.

Why do dolphins
swim in salt water?

Because pepper
makes them sneeze.

CHOO!

What should you do
with creased seals?

Use a seal-iron.

I've got two
octopuses that look
exactly alike.
I think they may
be itentacle.

Why is it easy to
weigh fish?
They come with
their own scales.

# Pirate Puns

Why did the
pirate cross
the sea?

To get to the
other tide.

What has eight eyes
and eight legs?

Eight pirates.

Where do pirates buy
Christmas presents?

**Arrrrrrrgos.**

How can you tell if
you're a pirate?

**If you arrr, you are.**

How much do pirates
pay for ear piercings?

**A buck-an-ear.**

When does a
pirate stand at
the very back end
of his ship?

**When he's being
stern.**

Where do pirates
go to the toilet?

**On the poop deck.**

How do pirates get
from ship to ship?

**By taxi crab.**

Why couldn't the
pirates play cards?

**Because the captain was
standing on the deck.**

What do you call
a pirate who is
missing an eye?

**Prate.**

Why don't pirates
get hungry on
desert islands?

**Because of all the sand
which is there.**

Where does a pirate
keep his treasure chest?

**Inside his treasure shirt.**

Is it expensive to
join a pirate crew?

**Yes – it'll cost you
an arm and a leg.**

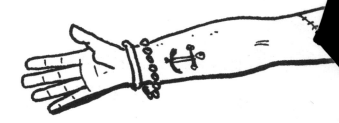

What lies shivering at the
bottom of the sea?

**A nervous wreck.**

Why is it really hard
to give up being a
pirate?

**You get hooked.**

Where do pirates
go to exercise?

**Our gym, lad!**

How do you spot a fuel-efficient pirate ship?

**It does sixty miles to the galleon.**

What do you call a pirate with two legs and two eyes?

**A trainee.**

# Animal Crackers

What do you call a
donkey with three legs?

**A wonkey.**

What do you call a
three-legged donkey
with one eye?

**A winky wonkey.**

Why should you
never play games
in the jungle?

Because there are
too many cheetahs.

How do you stop a
skunk smelling?
Hold its nose.

What do you get if
you sit under a cow?
A pat on the head.

What's a cow's
favourite party game?
Moosical chairs.

What kind of pet
makes the most noise?
A trumpet.

What do you call a
cow eating grass?

**A lawnmooer.**

How do cows
cheat in tests?

**They copy off
each udder.**

How do you make
instant elephant?

Open the packet, add
water – and run.

What do you give a
sick elephant?

A get-wellephant card.

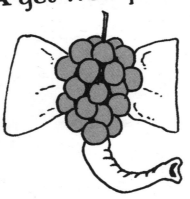

Why are elephants large,
wrinkled and grey?

Because if they were
small, smooth and green,
they'd be grapes.

What's big, grey and
doesn't matter?

**An irrelephant.**

Why are elephants
so wrinkled?
Well, have you ever
tried ironing one?

What's big,
grey and invisible?
**No elephants.**

What do you call a cat
with eight legs?

**An octopuss.**

What does a cat
put in its drink?

**Mice cubes.**

What do cats eat
for breakfast?

**Mice Krispies.**

What kinds of stories
do cats like?

**Furry tales.**

Did you hear about the
cat that swallowed a
ball of wool?

**She had mittens.**

What's the opposite
of a flabby tabby?

**An itty-bitty kitty.**

Why did the dog
smell of onions?

**It was a hot dog.**

Why don't dogs
drive cars?

**They can never find
a barking space.**

What did the dog
say to the bone?

**'It's been nice
gnawing you.'**

How do you stop a dog barking in the front garden?

Put it in the back garden.

Why does my dog keep scratching herself?

Because she's the only one who knows where she itches.

Why don't dogs
watch DVDs?

**They can only
press 'Paws'.**

Why can't Dalmatians
play hide-and-seek?
They're always spotted.

What do rabbits sing
at birthday parties?
'Hoppy birthday to you . . .'

What do you call a
rabbit with fleas?

**Bugs Bunny.**

Why did the rabbit
cross the road?
**It was the chicken's day off.**

Where can you find a
tortoise with no legs?

**Exactly where
you left it.**

What pet is
always smiling?

**A grinny pig.**

What's a mouse's
favourite game?

**Hide-and-squeak.**

What goes
'hiss, swish,
hiss, swish'?

**A windscreen
viper.**

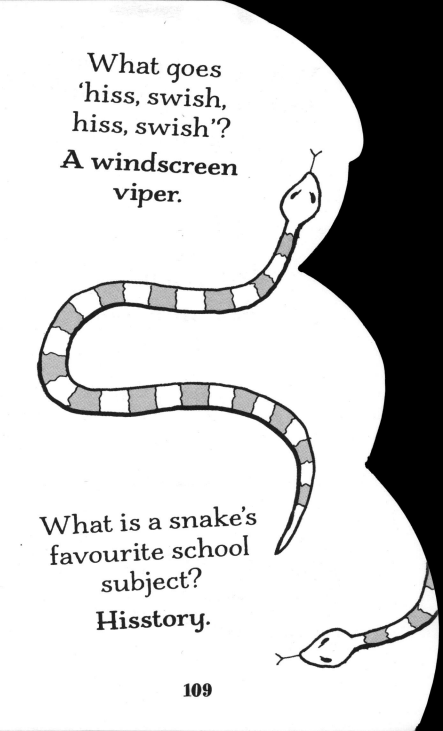

What is a snake's
favourite school
subject?

**Hisstory.**

What swings through
the trees and tastes
good with milk?

**A chocolate chimp
cookie.**

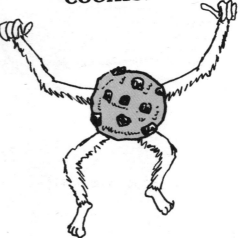

What kind of key do
you use to open
a banana?

**A monkey.**

Why do monkeys
have big nostrils?

Because they've got
big fingers.

Where do baby
apes sleep?

In apricots.

How do chimpanzees
make toast?

They put a slice of bread
under a gorilla.

Can chimpanzees fly?
No, but hot air
baboons can.

How do you fix a
broken chimpanzee?

With a monkey
wrench.

What do you call an
exploding monkey?

**A ba-boom!**

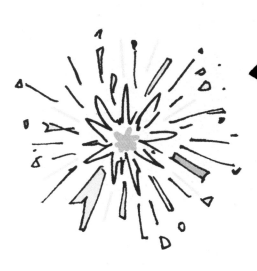

What do you give a
grumpy gorilla for its
birthday?

**I'm not sure, but you'd
better hope he likes it.**

Where do frogs keep
their money?

**In a river bank.**

What do you get if
you cross a frog with
a fizzy drink?

**Croaka-Cola.**

What does a frog eat
with a burger?
**French flies.**

What do frogs eat
for breakfast?
**Coco Hops.**

What is a frog's
favourite flower?
**A croakus.**

What happens
when a duck flies
upside down?

**It quacks up.**

Why are birds
so great?

**Because they always
suck seed.**

Where do birds
go to eat?

**A nestaurant.**

What do you call
a woodpecker
with no beak?

**A headbanger.**

What do birds say at
Halloween?
**Trick or tweet?**

What do you call a chicken staring at a lettuce?

**Chicken sees a salad.**

'Why have you bought all those birds?'

**'They were going cheep.'**

How do you find out
the price of a sheep?
**Just scan its baa-code.**

Where do sheep go to
get their fleece cut?
**The baa-baas.**

What do you give
a sick bird?
**Tweetment.**

What do you call
deer with no eyes?
No-eye deer.

What do you call a
deer with no eyes
and no legs?
Still no-eye deer.

What do you call
bears with no ears?

B.

PARDON?

My pony only wants
to be ridden after dark,
which is really annoying.
She's a total night mare.

How do you move a really heavy pig?

**With a pork-lift truck.**

How do you fit lots of pigs on a small farm?

**Build a styscraper.**

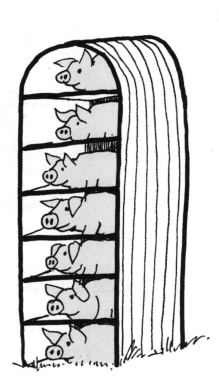